Bad Cats

Published by Statics (London) Ltd.
41 Standard Road, London NW10 6HF
Copyright © 1995 by Rick Stromoski

Printed in England by HPH Print Ltd.
Royal London Estate, 29 North Acton Road, London NW10 6PE.

ISBN 1-873922-38-8

STATICS BOOKS

Bad Cats

—stroMoski—

Rick was born on Christmas day 1958, the seventh in a family of twelve children. Growing up in such a large family gave Rick a special sense of humour that he has expressed through his drawings ever since childhood. His illustrations for humorous greetings cards have gained him nine nominations for the prestigious Louie Awards, winning on four occasions. Originally from New Jersey, U.S.A, Rick and his wife Danna, their baby girl Molly, along with their cat Crusty, now live in the historic district of Suffield, Connecticut.

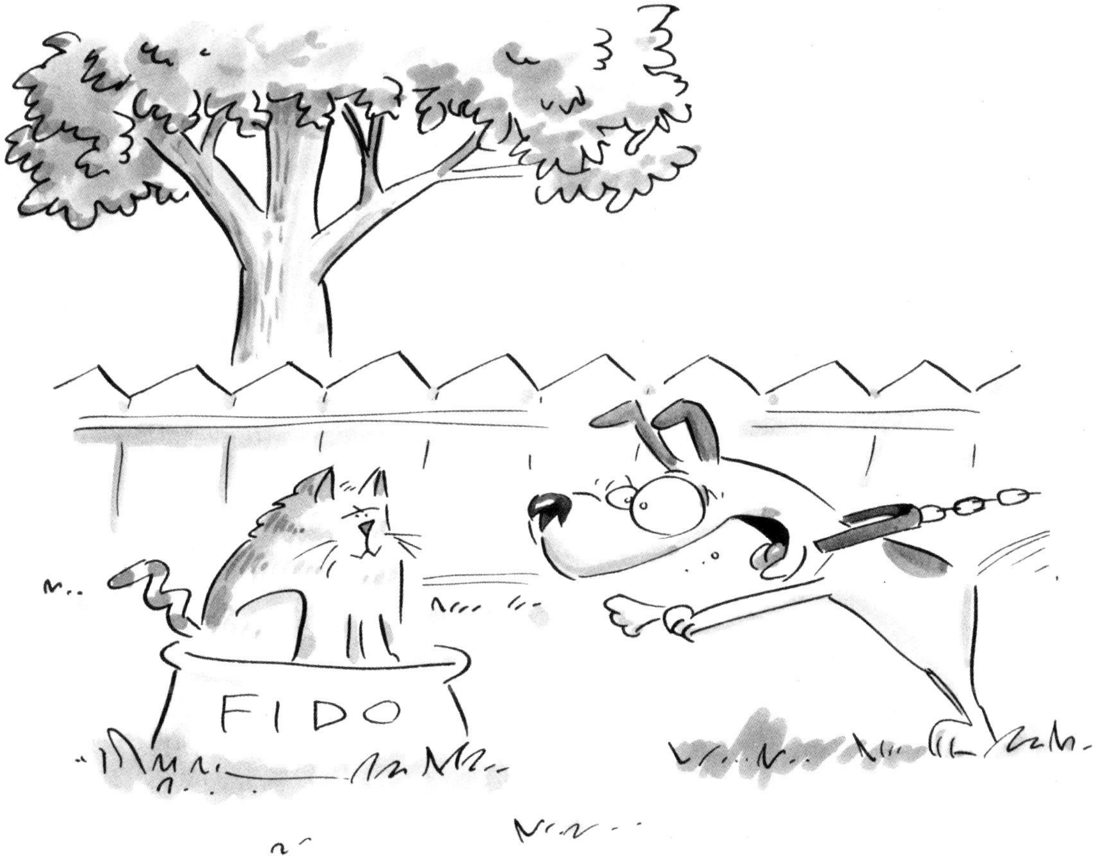
FIDO

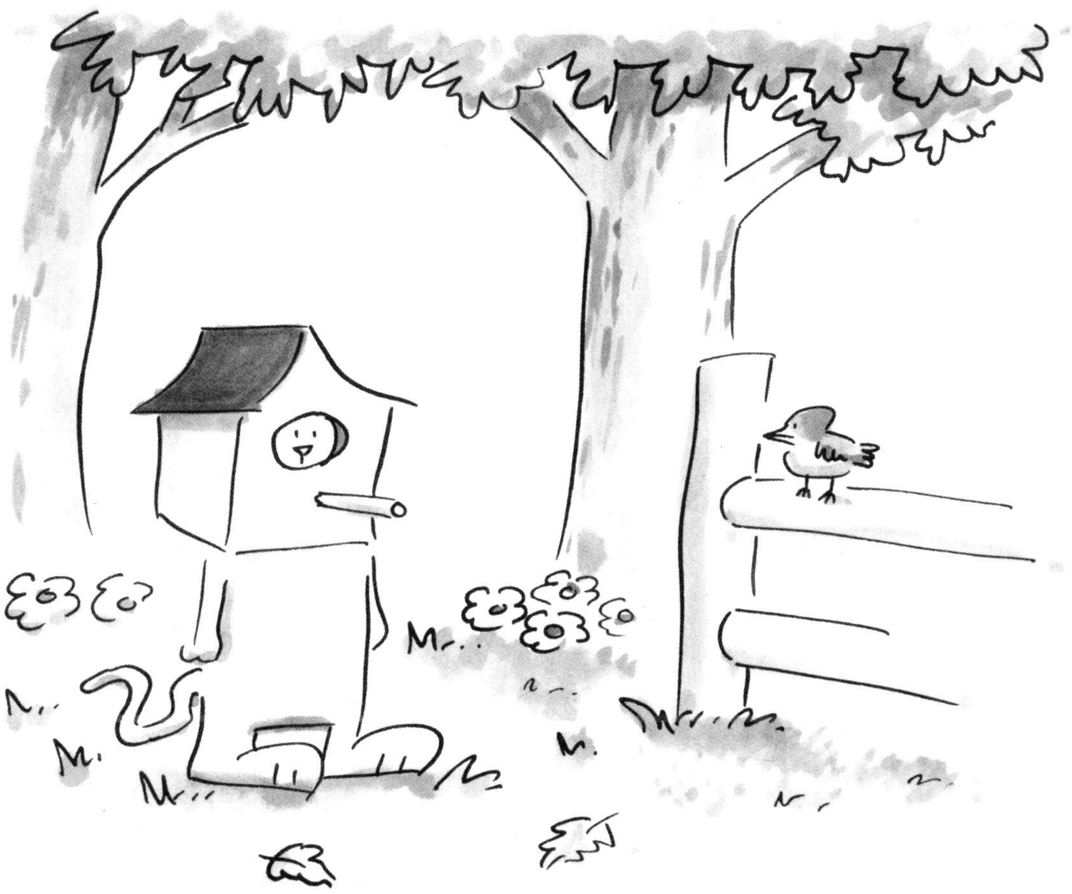

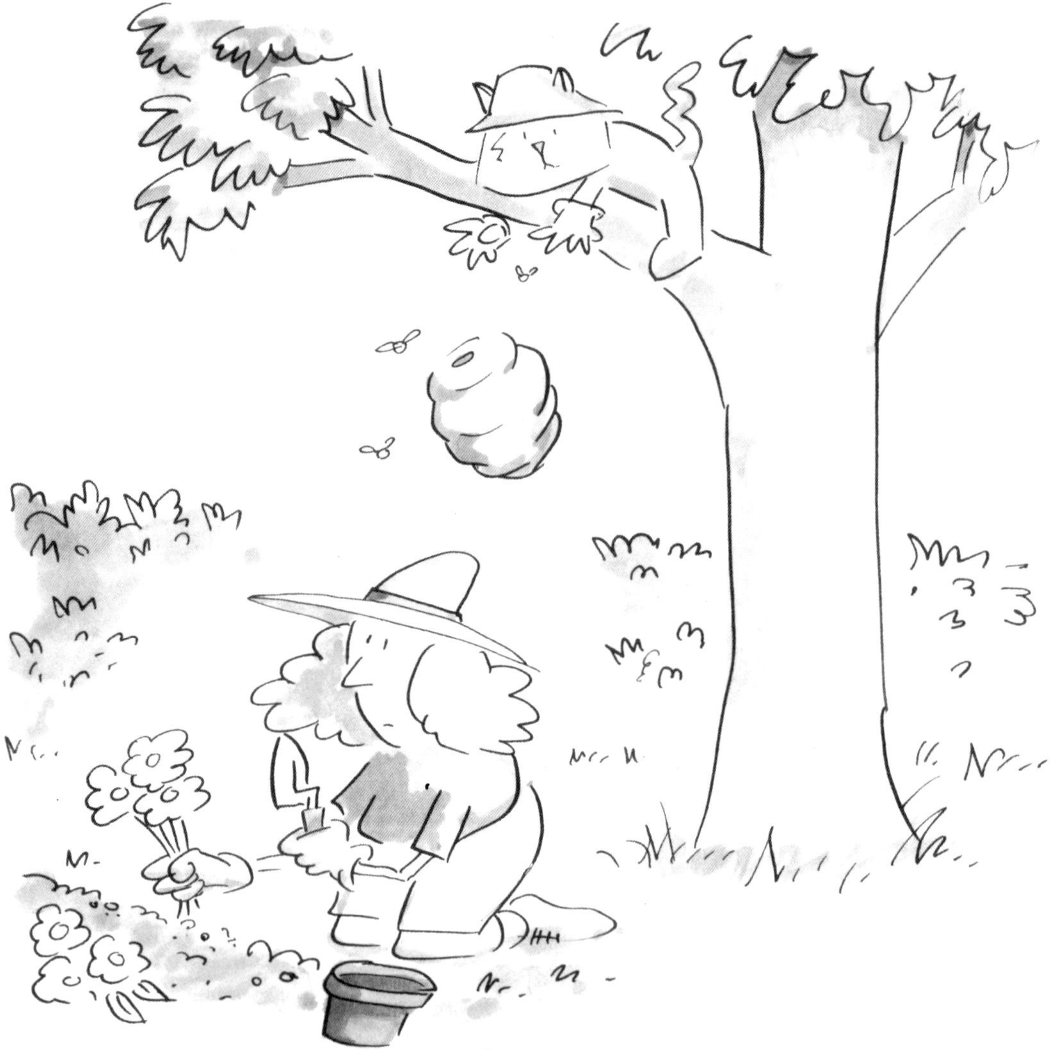